70 Classic QUILTING PATTERNS

Ready-to-Use Designs and Instructions

Gwen Marston
and
Joe Cunningham

DOVER PUBLICATIONS, INC.
New York

This book is dedicated to Mary Schafer,
whom we consider to be America's greatest living quiltmaker.

Published in Canada by General Publishing Company, Ltd.,
30 Lesmill Road, Don Mills, Toronto, Ontario.
Published in the United Kingdom by Constable and Company, Ltd.,
10 Orange Street, London WC2H 7EG.

70 Classic Quilting Patterns: Ready-to-Use Designs and Instructions
is a new work, first published by Dover Publications, Inc., in 1987.

All drawings by Marston and Cunningham.

International Standard Book Number: 0-486-25474-7

Manufactured in the United States of America
Dover Publications, Inc., 31 East 2nd Street, Mineola, N.Y. 11501

Introduction

Studying old quilts and making new ones has led us to believe that the choice and execution of the quilting designs is as important as any part of quiltmaking. Sometimes, the quilting makes the quilt, for rich, thorough quilting can make a plain quilt seem fancy. The opposite is also true—too little quilting can make even a fancy quilt seem plain.

Over the years we have collected and used hundreds of quilting patterns from many sources. The selection presented here offers a wide range of designs from small to large and from simple spot motifs to elaborate repeating borders. The designs come from four sources. The patterns on Plates 1–18 were designed by our friend and mentor, nationally known quiltmaker Mary Schafer. Those in Plates 19–24 were collected by Mary's friend Betty Harriman, a great quiltmaker from Bunceton, Missouri. When Betty died in 1971, Mary acquired all of her patterns and unfinished work and has since completed nineteen of Betty's started quilts. Plates 25–28 show a few of the patterns Gwen was given by her Mennonite quilt teachers at the Zion Mennonite Church in Hubbard, Oregon, and the rest of the patterns were either designed or collected by us. We hope that you find our selection useful and beautiful.

General Instructions for Quilting

Once you have completed your quilt top, it is a good idea to hang it up for a few days. Look at it and think about different ways to quilt it; browse through the pages of this book and see how various patterns work with your quilt design. The chances are that you can quilt your top in many ways, all equally effective. Between the patterns in this book and your finished quilt are two steps: transferring the patterns to the quilt top and quilting them.

Transferring the Pattern to Your Quilt Top

After all the fun and excitement of working with colors and patterns and seeing your quilt top come together, transferring the pattern can seem like a tedious job. It is important, however, to the overall success of your quilt, so we will try to make the process as easy as possible.

While there are many products and techniques available to help you mark your quilt top, you probably already have almost everything you need on hand. The only two unusual tools we use are:

White and silver Berol Verithin pencils.—We have tried many pens and pencils, soap, soapstones, carbon paper and more for transferring, but find that these pencils, which can be purchased from drafting-supply stores or art shops, are the best for us. They hold a sharp point for a long time, do not stain the fabric, and the line disappears from the top as you quilt. Any residue comes out with the first washing.

A homemade light table.—This is merely a piece of glass with a light source below. We have improvised setups with a piece of picture glass and a living-room lamp. Now we use one of our storm windows for the glass. The most important part of your setup will be a piece of plain white paper taped to the glass to diffuse the light and give you a larger area on which to work. We sometimes use three or four layers of paper, until we can see both the pattern and the lines we are drawing.

For quilts with white or unbleached muslin spaces to be quilted, all you need to do is slip the quilting pattern under the quilt top and trace the lines directly onto the fabric. The silver pencil works best for this, although a regular hard lead pencil such as a #3 drafting pencil will do. Maintain a sharp point and mark as lightly as you can. The most important thing to remember is to keep the lines just dark enough to see.

Most quilts require another marking system. Colored or printed fabrics call for templates (fine for simple designs) or the light table (best for complex designs). Each technique has its advantages: templates require a minimum of fuss while light tables can solve problems no other technique can.

Templates can be made of cardboard, plastic, sandpaper, even sheet metal. We like cardboard the best since we always seem to have it in the house. Plastic can work as well as or better than cardboard, particularly if you plan to reuse the template, but it is much more expensive. If you are like us, you will rarely use the same quilting pattern twice, so cardboard is perfectly satisfactory.

To make your own template, cut the pattern from the book, leaving at least ¼″ (6 mm) of blank paper all around. Glue the pattern to a piece of lightweight cardboard. If you do not want to cut up the book or you want to change the design in some way, trace it onto lightweight paper and glue the tracing to cardboard. Use an X-ACTO knife to cut around the shape. For the inside lines you must cut slots, leaving the ends connected as shown in *Diagram 1*. Obviously, this technique is best suited for simpler designs. Once again, it is important to maintain a sharp point on your pencil and to mark lightly. With a little practice you will learn to drag the pencil at the proper angle to keep the fabric from bunching up in front of it.

Diagram 1

To make your own light table, find a piece of glass large enough to span the gap left when you remove a leaf from your dining-room table. If your table does not have removable leaves, any similar space, such as the space between a couch and coffee table, will do. Place a lamp beneath the glass as shown in *Diagram 2* and tape a piece of plain white paper to the glass to diffuse the light. Lay the pattern on the paper, then the quilt top over all. If the light source is so bright that you cannot see where you have marked and

where you haven't, place another layer of paper under the pattern.

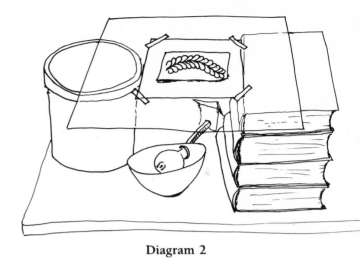

Diagram 2

Tools and Materials for Quilting

Quilting Needles
Needles made for hand quilting, called "betweens," are available in sewing-supply stores. They are short, sturdy needles with small eyes and come in sizes 7–10, with 7 being the largest. The different brands vary in length, some brands being longer than average, some shorter. It is difficult to say which size or brand is best, since this is a matter of personal preference. Try several sizes and brands until you find the one you like best.

Quilting Thread
Quilting thread is stronger than thread used for most hand sewing and usually has some kind of a slippery coating so that it can better withstand the tension and friction of hand quilting. Before commercially coated threads were available, quilters often kept a cake of beeswax handy and coated their own. We have found that 100% cotton quilting thread ravels less than blends or all polyester.

Thimble
The instructions given in this book are for a single thimble placed on the middle finger of your sewing hand—your right hand if you are right-handed. We have found that nickel-silver thimbles work best, but regular metal thimbles work well if they have deep, sharp-edged pits to catch the needle. There are many other types of thimbles on the market, including leather thimbles and small paddle-like implements designed to replace the thimble. Also, some quilters prefer to use a thimble on both hands. Try the method described here, then try others to see which you like best.

Scissors
The only scissors you need when you are quilting are small thread-clippers. Embroidery scissors or other small shears work fine.

Pins

Pins used in a quilting frame undergo severe strain, so large, strong pins are best. Large straight pins with plastic heads have become so popular for this that they are now often called "quilter's pins." One or two small boxes should be all you need.

Batting

Hand quilting requires a fairly thin layer of batting, or stuffing. Too thick a batt means large stitches and difficult quilting. Bonded polyester batts are the most popular for several reasons: ease of handling, high loft, ease of needling and stability. Stability means large areas of the quilt can be left unquilted. Wool batts are available which have many of the same characteristics as bonded polyester batts but which require more care in cleaning and closer quilting. Cotton batting is the most difficult to handle and requires the closest quilting, but it gives the "old-fashioned" look. Our favorite batt is the Cotton Classic, made by the Fairfield Corporation. It is 80% cotton and 20% polyester, combining the best properties of both with few drawbacks. Batting comes in different sizes, so you should check the dimensions of your quilt top before you shop for a batting.

Quilting Frame or Hoop

While it is possible to quilt three layers of material together without having them secured to any kind of frame, it is much easier if the three layers are held taut. There are three main approaches to this: the full-size frame, which is a simple frame as large as the quilt; the roller frame, in which the quilt is rolled like a scroll; and the quilting hoop, which is like an oversize embroidery hoop. Each has its advantages. The roller frame and the hoop require that the layers of the quilt be basted together to keep them from shifting as you work on various parts. With either of these you must start in the center and work outward to eliminate fullness and wrinkles. On the full-size frame there is no basting and you quilt from the outside to the center.

Preparing to Quilt

Whether you quilt without a hoop, with a hoop or in a roller frame, we feel that the best way to start is to assemble the three layers of your quilt "sandwich" in a full-size frame. A quilt that is basted in the full-size frame will be secure against shifting, bunching or distortion, as one basted on the floor cannot be. This means you will have less trouble quilting and your quilt will look better when it is done. Here is how to make and use a full-size frame.

Go to the nearest lumberyard and buy four 1″ by 2″ (2.5 cm by 5 cm) pine boards and four 2″ (5 cm) C-clamps. Two of the boards should be about 12″ (30.5 cm) longer than your quilt top and the other two should be about 12″ (30.5 cm) wider. Measure each board and mark the exact center.

For each board, cut a strip of sturdy fabric about 4″ (10 cm) wide and as long as the board. Fold the long outside edges of the strip toward the center until they meet, then fold the strip in half lengthwise (*Diagram 3*). Lay each strip on its matching board with the center fold extending ½″ (1.3 cm) over the edge, then use a staple gun to staple the strip to the board every 2″ (5 cm) (*Diagram 4*).

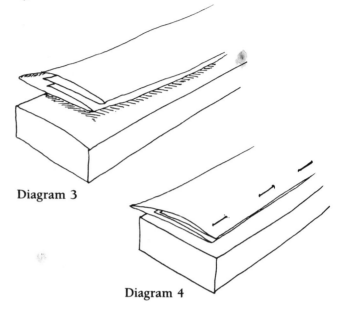

Diagram 3

Diagram 4

That's it. The only other things you will need will be some sturdy pins to pin it all together and straight-backed chairs to rest the assembled frame on.

Arrange the four chairs about where the corners of the quilt will be. Rest two matching boards, or "stretchers," parallel to each other with the fabric up and in, as in *Diagram 5*. Lay the other two boards, or "rollers," across the stretchers. The backing material for your quilt should be approximately 3″ (7.5 cm) longer and wider than the top. Find the center of each end of the back and pin the ends to the fabric strips of the rollers, matching the centers to the center marks on the boards. Make sure the seams of the backing are facing upward, or they will end up on the outside of your quilt. Stretch the backing out toward the end of each roller and pin it taut. Using a quilting needle and quilting thread, whipstitch the backing to the roller fabric with stitches about ⅓″ (8 mm) long.

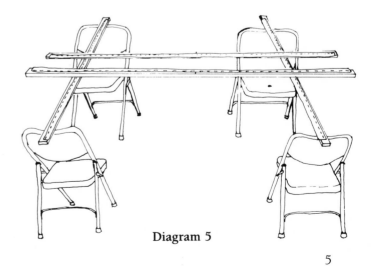

Diagram 5

Now you can clamp the frame together with the C-clamps, pulling the backing fabric taut. Line the stretchers up so that the backing can be pinned to them (*Diagram 6*). Pin the backing about every 2" (5 cm) along each stretcher. You should now have a trampoline-like frame, with the backing sewn to the rollers, pulled taut and smooth with seam or seams up and pinned to the stretchers.

Carefully unroll the batting and spread it over the backing. Starting in one corner, line up two adjacent sides. Smooth the batting carefully until there are no wrinkles, using a yardstick if necessary to reach the center. Cut off the excess batting that is hanging down on the two opposite sides.

Finally, lay the quilt top on the batting with the seams down. Spread and smooth it out. When you have it centered on the backing, pin along its edge every 2" (5 cm) or 3" (7.5 cm) starting from one corner and working all the way around (*Diagram 7*). Pull the top taut, but do not pull hard enough to distort the blocks or borders. When the top is installed properly it will be wrinkle-free and square.

If you are going to quilt your quilt in the frame you can simply start quilting—no basting is required. This is one of the chief advantages of the full-size frame. Most likely, however, you will choose to quilt it in a roller frame or in a hoop, in which case you can now begin basting.

Begin basting with a quilting needle and a long thread. Tie a knot, then baste across the quilt from right to left (if you are right-handed), with lines about 4" (10 cm) apart. The stitches should be about 1" (2.5 cm) long. When you have done three or four lines and can reach no further, begin basting toward yourself with lines about 4" (10 cm) apart, creating a grid of basting lines all around the edge of the quilt. In order to reach to the center you must roll the quilt on the rollers.

Rolling the finished part to reach the center of the quilt must be done the same whether you are basting or quilting. Unclamp both ends of one roller and unpin the backing from the stretchers on each side far enough to

allow rolling up the basted part. It is easiest to roll with two people, one for each stretcher. Brace the stretcher against your thigh, roll the roller as far as you have basted or quilted, pull it taut and reclamp it. Check the underside as you work and after you roll to make sure that there are no wrinkles. Continue to baste or quilt as far as you can reach, then unclamp, roll and reclamp again. Repeat this process until you reach the center. When you are done, your quilt will resemble a scroll.

How to Quilt

The quilting stitch is one of the simplest in all of sewing—a plain running stitch. It seems, however, that if you ask ten quilters how it is done you will get at least ten answers—most of which will be confusing and contradictory. Don't be discouraged; it truly is not hard, requiring only a few hours of practice to learn and one quilting project to learn well. There are three parts to hand quilting: getting started, the stitch itself and ending the quilting line.

You can start a line of quilting in one of two ways: with or without a knot. We prefer to avoid knots when we can. To do this, thread a needle with about 30" (76 cm) of thread—twice as much as you need for one quilting line. Start quilting, leaving about half of the thread as a tail on top of the quilt. When you have quilted the line and finished and snipped the thread, return to the tail and thread it onto your needle. If there is no quilting line handy, slip the needle between the quilt layers and come up on a line to be quilted. Proceed as before. In other words, simply quilt with both ends of the thread.

Sometimes you will find yourself without another quilting line nearby, in which case it may be necessary to tie a knot. Tie a small knot near the end of an 18" (46 cm) length of thread. Insert the needle through the top and between the layers of the quilt sandwich about 1" (2.5 cm)

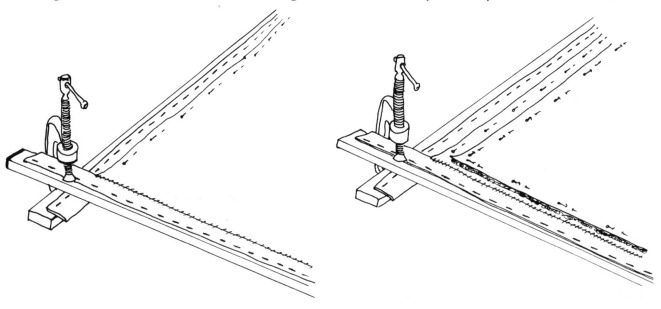

Diagram 6   Diagram 7

away from where you plan to start quilting. Bring the needle up at the point where you want to begin (*Diagram 8*). Gently tug the thread until the knot pops through the top and lodges between the layers (*Diagram 9*). Now you are ready to start quilting. It is always easiest to quilt toward you, so be sure to pick a line that will let you quilt that way.

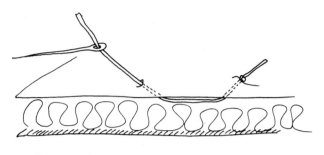

Diagram 8

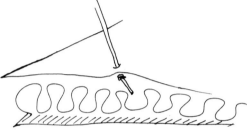

Diagram 9

If you are right-handed, you should have a thimble on the middle finger of your right hand; reverse that if you are left-handed. The hand with the thimble is your sewing hand and stays on top of the quilt; the other hand stays below the quilt. Press upward slightly with the index finger of the hand underneath, raising the point where you want to start. Stand the needle straight up on top of the index finger and let go of it. From this point on you will not touch the needle with your fingers, only with the thimble (*Diagram 10*).

"Stand" the thimble on the needle and press the needle down flat to the quilt for the first—and most difficult—stitch (*Diagram 11*). The first time you try this, the needle will pop out and get away from you; in fact, it might do this the first dozen times. Don't worry; in an hour or two you will be able to take that first stitch every time.

Now that you have taken a stitch you could pull the needle through and start over, but we prefer to get as many stitches on the needle as we can handle (five or six is usually the limit). You take these stitches by pushing on the needle with the end of the thimble until you can feel the point of the needle with the hand underneath (*Diagram 12*). Then, angle the needle the other way to make the point of the needle barely come through to the surface (*Diagram 13*). Repeat for another stitch. When you have several stitches on the needle, pull it all the way through and pull the thread tight. Pull just tightly enough to remove all the slack, but not so tight that the fabric bunches or wrinkles.

Diagram 10

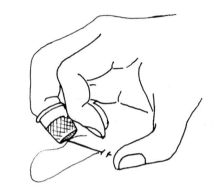

Diagram 11

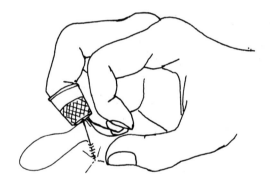

Diagram 12

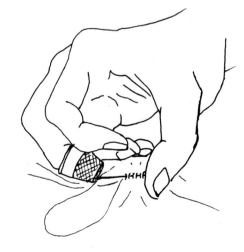

Diagram 13

Because you will be feeling the point of the needle with your thumb underneath the quilt, it will eventually become sore, as will your thumb on top. The more you quilt, the more tolerance you will have for this. Many methods have been devised to protect your hands from the needle, such as using a thimble on each hand, or using some other tool to push and deflect the needle. You may want to investigate one of these alternate methods, but we have quilted many quilts without finding any of them necessary.

When you have reached the end of the quilting line or have run out of thread, it is time to make the end of the thread disappear inconspicuously. If you are near a seam, you can run the needle between the layers and come up on the seam. Otherwise you must run the needle between the layers back the way you came or to another quilting line and come up on a quilting stitch (*Diagram 14*). Do not take a back stitch, but take a stitch around one thread as shown (*Diagram 15*). Repeat this procedure along the seam. Run the needle between the layers for about 1″ (2.5 cm), then back through to the surface. Carefully clip the thread and let the tail slip back below the surface fabric.

The size of your quilting stitches will vary with the materials you use and the amount of practice you have had. More important than the size is consistency and neatness. Whatever size your stitches, try to make them all the same.

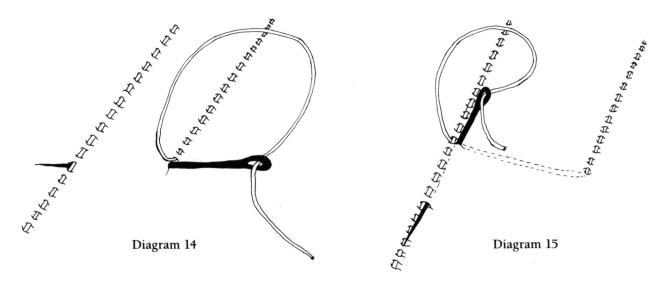

Diagram 14   Diagram 15

Plate 1

Plate 2

Plate 3

Plate 4

Plate 5

Center

To complete design, rotate pattern, matching center lines.

Center

Plate 6

Tape pattern pieces together at broken line

Center

Plate 7

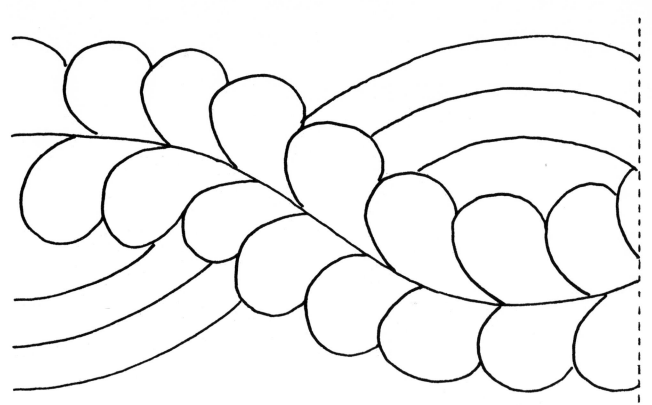

Tape pattern pieces together at broken line.

Plate 8

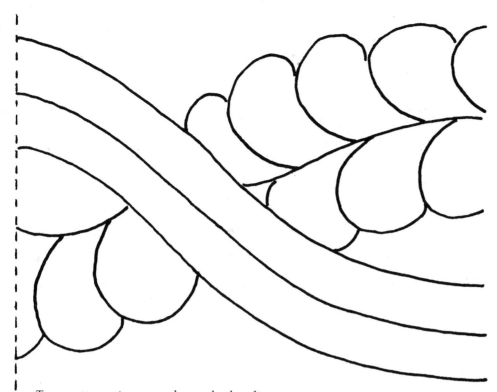

Tape pattern pieces together at broken line.

Plate 9

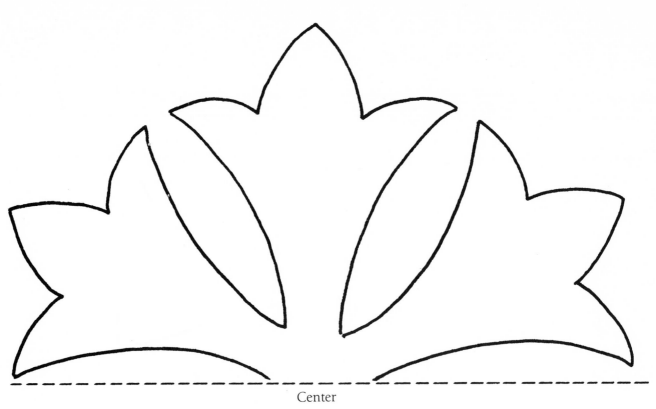

Center

Reverse pattern along center line to complete design.

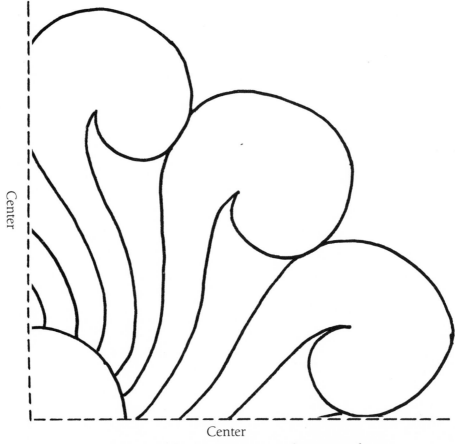

Center

Center

To complete design, rotate pattern, matching center lines.

Plate 10

Center

Reverse pattern along center line to complete design.

Plate 11

Reverse pattern along center line to complete design.

Plate 12

Center

Center

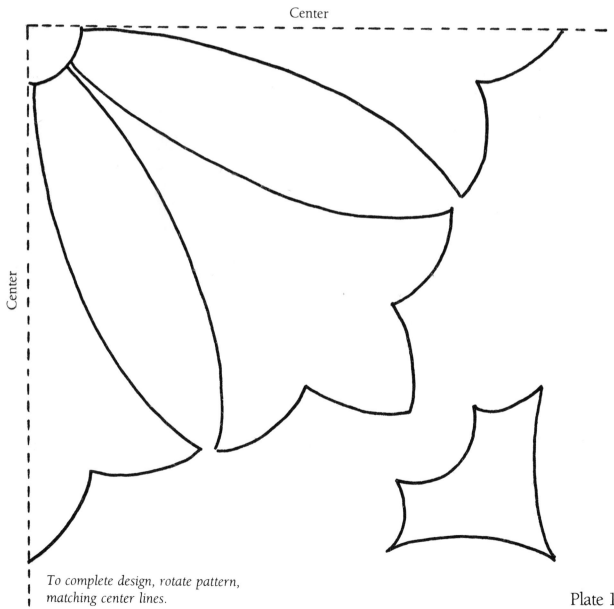

*To complete design, rotate pattern,
matching center lines.*

Plate 13

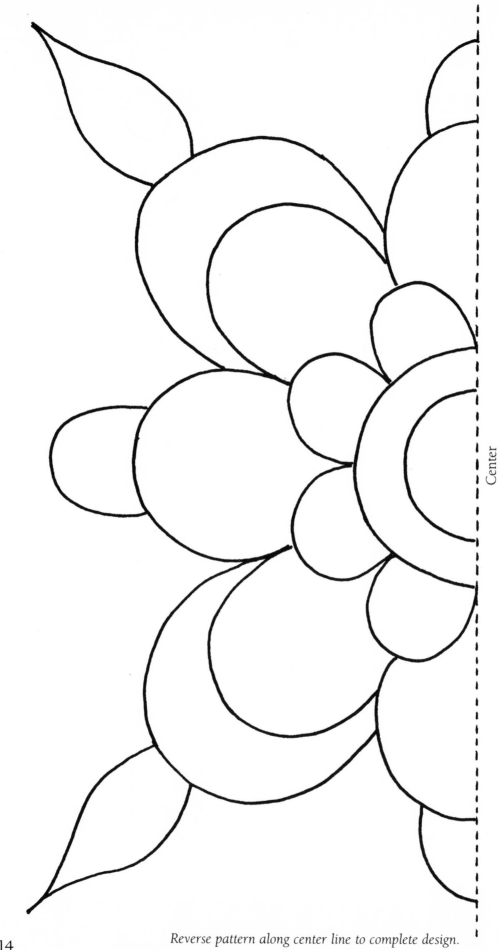

Center

Plate 14

Reverse pattern along center line to complete design.

Center

Reverse pattern along center line to complete design.

Plate 15

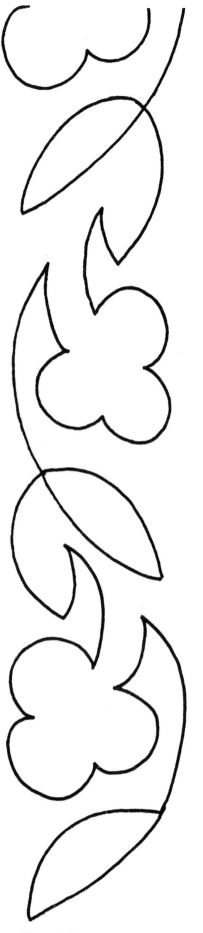
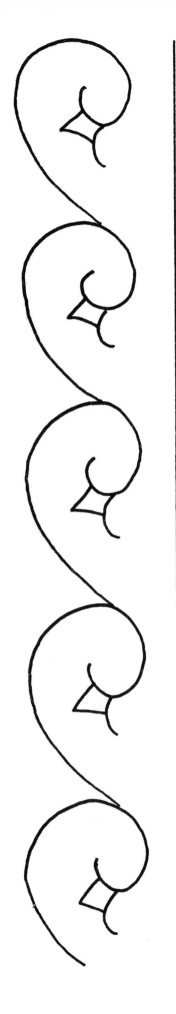
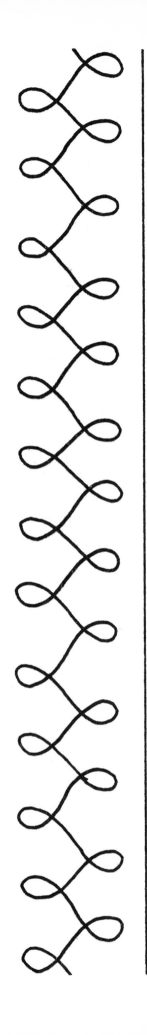

Plate 16

Plate 17

Center

Center

Plate 18   *To complete design, rotate pattern, matching center lines.*

Plate 19

Plate 20

Plate 21

Plate 22

Plate 23

Center
Reverse pattern along center line to complete design.

Plate 24

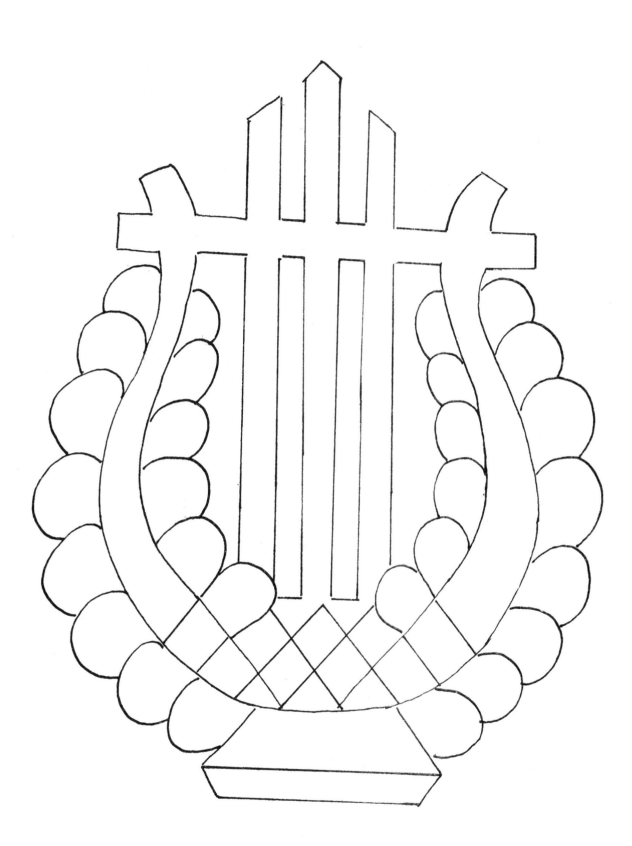

Plate 25

*Tape pattern pieces
together at broken line.*

*Tape pattern pieces
together at broken line.*

Plate 26

Plate 27

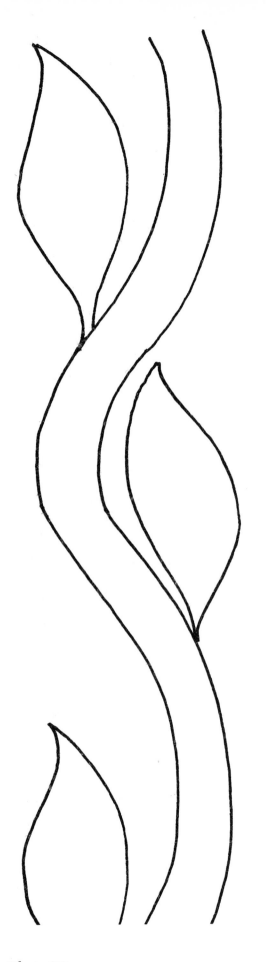

Plate 28

Plate 29

Plate 30

Plate 31

A ————————————   B —————————

Plate 32   *Tape to pattern on Plate 33, matching letters.*

Tape to pattern on Plate 32, matching letters.

A   B

Plate 33

Plate 34

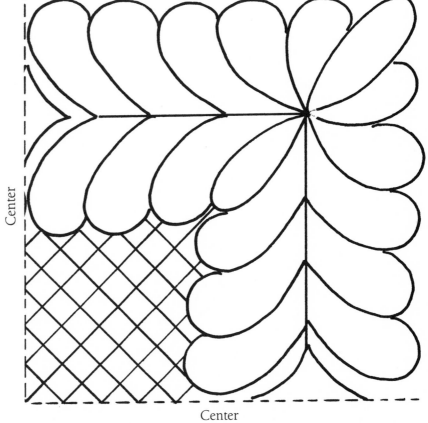

To complete design, rotate pattern, matching center lines.

Center

Center

Plate 35

A

Tape pattern pieces together, matching letters.

B

Center

Reverse pattern along center line to complete design.

Plate 36

A

Tape pattern pieces together, matching letters.

B

Center

Reverse pattern along center line to complete design.

Plate 37

Plate 38

Tape to pattern on Plate 38 at broken line.

Plate 39

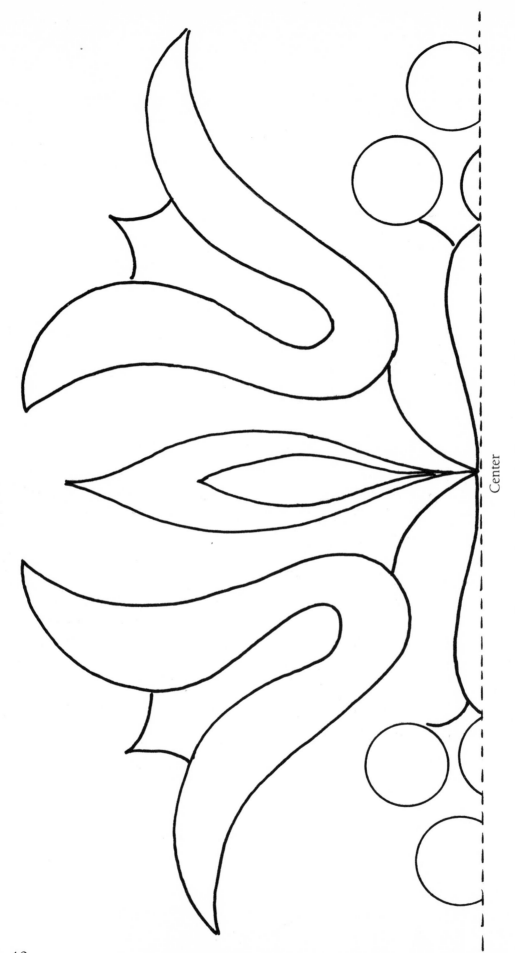

Plate 40

Center

Reverse pattern along center line to complete design.

Tape pattern pieces together at broken line.

Tape pattern pieces together at broken line.

Plate 41

Plate 42

Center

Reverse pattern along center line to complete design.

Plate 43

Center

Reverse pattern along center line to complete design.

Plate 44